The Story of a Special Day
Volume 299

October
25

The 298th day of the year (299th in leap years).
There are 67 days remaining until the end of the year.

by Michael Dobson

Timespinner
Press

This book is also available in e-book form for Kindle, e-pub
devices, and other formats from your favorite online booksellers.

For more information about the series, about us, or about your
special day, please email us at editor@timespinnerpress.com.

Look for other volumes in *The Story of a Special Day,* coming
often. See www.timespinnerpress.com for details and for the most
recent information.

Table of Contents

For the definition of "O.S.," "CE," and "BCE" used with some dates , see the section "On Names and Dates."

Cover: ""Charge of the Light Cavalry Brigade, 25th October 1854, under Major General the Earl of Cardigan," by William Simpson and E. Walker — for the EVENT OF THE DAY.

Quote of the Day

"We few, we happy few, we band of brothers.
For he to-day that sheds his blood with me,
Shall be my brother; be he ne'er so vile,
This day shall gentle his condition:
And gentlemen in England, now a-bed,
Shall think themselves accurs'd, they were not here,
And hold their manhoods cheap, whiles any speaks,
That fought with us upon Saint Crispin's day."

William Shakespeare, *Henry V*
speech given by the king prior to the Battle of Agincourt,
which took place on St. Crispin's Day, October 25, 1415.

Today in History

October 25

The Charge of the Light Brigade, by Caton Woodville

Event of the Day
The Charge of the Light Brigade

In one of the most famous mistakes in military history, The Charge of the Light Brigade occurred on October 25, 1854, during the Battle of Balaclava, an attempt by combined English, French, and Turkish forces during the Crimean War to besiege the strategically vital Russian port of Sevastopol, located on the Black Sea.

The British forces, commanded by Field Marshal the Right Honorable Lord Raglan, were responsible for the right flank of the siege, and occupied the nearby port of Balaclava with a force of about 4,500. Seeing the small British garrison as vulnerable, a Russian force of some 25,000 soldiers under the command of General Pavel Liprandi (Павел Петрович Липранди) attacked, but were held back by the Scottish 93rd (Highland) Regiment, which became known as the "Thin Red Line." A charge by British heavy cavalry (partially armored) pushed the Russians onto defense.

At that point, Lord Raglan decided to send his fast-moving and unarmored light cavalry, consisting of about 670 horse soldiers, in pursuit of a retreating Russian artillery battery, a role for which light cavalry are well suited. However, the orders (admittedly vague) were misinterpreted as they moved down the chain of command, and instead of being sent after the retreating battery, the Light Brigade was ordered instead to make a direct frontal assault on a *different* artillery battery, one that was well prepared and fully dug in.

The reasons for this error are still debated. Besides ambiguity in Raglan's original order, there is the possible role of he man who conveyed the order from Raglan, Captain Louis Nolan. Nolan was killed early in the charge, possibly after realizing the mistake and trying to stop it. Another possibility is the conflict between the overall cavalry commander, the Earl of Lucan, and the Light Brigade commander, Lord Cardigan (after whom the cardigan sweater is named). The two men were brothers in law who hated each other.

Finally, there was Lord Cardigan himself, a man known for arrogance and incompetence (one of his commanding officers had once called him "constitutionally unfit for command").

Although it was obvious that "someone had blundered," no protest was raised, and the charge began with Lord Cardigan in the lead. The Light Brigade rode into heavy fire and even reached the Russian guns, but without backup from Lucan's heavy cavalry, they were rapidly repulsed, and retreated with 118 men killed, 127 wounded, and about 60 taken prisoner. Only 195 of the original Light Brigade returned with their horses, including Cardigan.

Lucan's heavy cavalry didn't charge at all, leaving his brother-in-law's force completely exposed. Although Lord Cardigan led the charge,

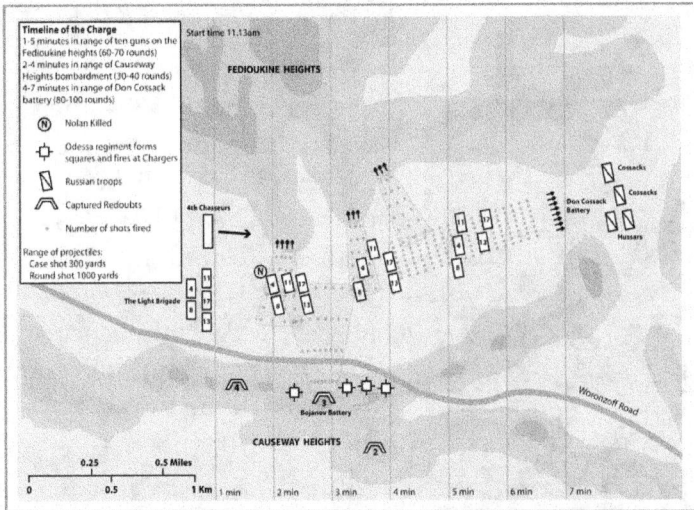

Timeline of the Charge of the Light Brigade

some argue that he actually fled the scene before the Light Brigade hit the Russian line. After the battle, Cardigan boarded his yacht in Balaclava harbor to have a champagne dinner.

Initially Cardigan was hailed as a hero, and his brother-in-law and superior officer Lucan was recalled in disgrace, possibly as a scapegoat for Raglan. However, reports from numerous Light Brigade survivors about his real conduct eroded his reputation. He remained a personal favorite of the Prince of Wales, and retired to his country estate.

The Poem

Alfred, Lord Tennyson

On December 9, 1854, the weekly London newspaper *The Examiner* published a poem by Great Britain's Poet Laureate, Alfred, Lord Tennyson: *The Charge of the Light Brigade*. Famous for such lines as "Into the valley of Death / Rode the six hundred," the poem — which Tennyson wrote in just a few minutes after reading a newspaper account of the Charge — became hugely popular, and remains one of the great classics of English literature. The poem's hoofbeat cadence and patriotic tone contrast strongly with his unflinching portrayal of the horrors of war.

Alfred Tennyson was the first person in British history to be elevated to the peerage on the strength of his writing; he was made Baron Tennyson by Queen Victoria. He is the ninth most frequently quoted writer in *The Oxford Dictionary of Quotations*.

Thomas Edison made a recording of Tennyson reciting his own poem on a wax cylinder in 1890; it can be found on the Wikipedia page devoted to the poem or on YouTube at http://www.youtube.com/watch?v=MkqUq26z1CE.

The Charge of the Light Brigade

Alfred, Lord Tennyson

I

Half a league, half a league,
Half a league onward,
All in the valley of Death
Rode the six hundred.
"Forward, the Light Brigade!
Charge for the guns!" he said.
Into the valley of Death
Rode the six hundred.

II

"Forward, the Light Brigade!"
Was there a man dismayed?
Not though the soldier knew
Someone had blundered.
Theirs not to make reply,
Theirs not to reason why,
Theirs but to do and die.
Into the valley of Death
Rode the six hundred.

III

Cannon to right of them,
Cannon to left of them,
Cannon in front of them
Volleyed and thundered;
Stormed at with shot and shell,
Boldly they rode and well,
Into the jaws of Death,
Into the mouth of hell
Rode the six hundred.

IV

Flashed all their sabres bare,
Flashed as they turned in air
Sabring the gunners there,
Charging an army, while
All the world wondered.
Plunged in the battery-smoke
Right through the line they broke;
Cossack and Russian
Reeled from the sabre stroke
Shattered and sundered.
Then they rode back, but not
Not the six hundred.

V

Cannon to right of them,
Cannon to left of them,
Cannon behind them
Volleyed and thundered;
Stormed at with shot and shell,
While horse and hero fell.
They that had fought so well
Came through the jaws of Death,
Back from the mouth of hell,
All that was left of them,
Left of six hundred.

VI

When can their glory fade?
O the wild charge they made!
All the world wondered.
Honour the charge they made!
Honour the Light Brigade,
Noble six hundred!

King Henry V at the Battle of Agincourt, by Harry Payne

What Happened on October 25?

From the creation of great works of engineering and art, to devastating wars and natural disasters, thousands of years of history have left their mark on each and every day of the year. Here are some important events that occurred on October 25. (Items with a photo or illustration are boxed.)

1415 — Under the command of King Henry V, English longbowmen defeat a numerically superior French army in the **Battle of Agincourt**, a central event in William Shakespeare's play *Henry V*.

1760 — **George III becomes King of Great Britain.** His reign would see the American War of Independence and the defeat of Napoleon. After 1810, his eldest son became regent because the king had become permanently mentally ill.

1812 — The frigate USS *United States*, commanded by Stephen Decatur, **defeats and captures** HMS *Macedonian* in one of the most famous engagements of the War of 1812.

1940 — Benjamin O. Davis, Sr., becomes the **first African-American general** in the United States Army.

1944 — The Battle of Leyte Gulf, often cited as the **largest naval battle in history**, takes place in the Philippines from October 23-26, 1944, leading to a decisive Allied victory over the Japanese Navy.

1962 — During the **Cuban Missile Crisis**, Adlai Stevenson shows photographs to the UN Security Council proving Soviet missiles had been installed in Cuba.

1971 — The United Nations **gives the China seat** held by the Republic of China (Taiwan) **to the People's Republic of China**, terminating Taiwan's membership in that body.

1997 — The US and its Caribbean allies **invade Grenada** to depose Prime Minister Maurice Bishop, who was installing a Marxist dictatorship.

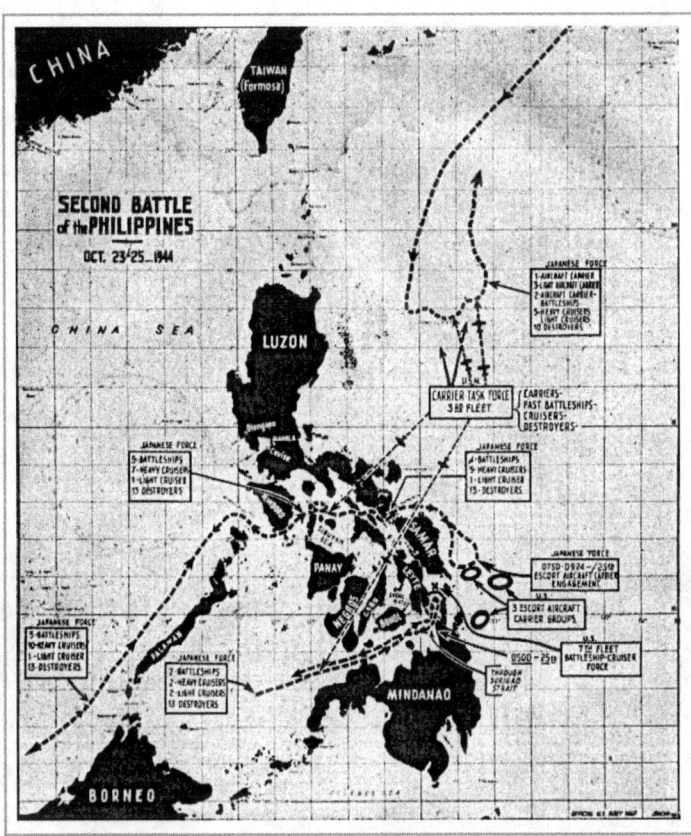

Map of the Battle of Leyte Gulf, US Navy *All Hands* Magazine

Quote of the Day

"Nothing is so useless as a general maxim."

Thomas Macaulay, poet and politician
born October 25, 1800

Births
and
Deaths

October 25

Portrait of Pablo Picasso by Juan Gris (1912).
Picasso was born on October 25, 1881.

Notable October 25 People

With the current world population at about seven billion people, on average about 19 million people also celebrate their birthdays on October 25 — and that isn't counting millions and millions who came before! No matter when you were born, you share your birthday with many special people whose accomplishments (and occasionally embarrassments) have been noted as part of history.

In this section, you'll meet fascinating people who share your birthday. They're organized by what they're famous for, and then in reverse chronological order from most recent to earliest. Those who are shown in photographs or artwork have a box around them. We don't have photos of everyone, so please forgive us if your favorite person is missing.

Some of these people you've heard of, others will be new to you, but they all make up an important part of the reason that October 25 is a truly special day!

Poster from the 1930 motion picture *With Byrd at the South Pole*

Who Was Born on October 25?

Art

Pablo Picasso, one of the most influential and important artists of the 20th century, co-founded the Cubist movement. *(1881) (Photo, page 8)*

Business and Technology

John Francis Dodge, automobile maker, co-founded Dodge Brothers Company, member of the Automotive Hall of Fame. *(1864)*

Exploration and Adventure

Rusty Schweickart, American astronaut who served as lunar module pilot on the Apollo 9 mission. *(1935)*

Richard E. Byrd, American naval officer and Medal of Honor winner noted for his polar expeditions. *(1888)*

Joseph Montferrand, French-Canadian logger and strong man who inspired the legendary figure "Big Joe Mufferaw" and "Big Joe," the mascot of the Canadian Football League's Ottawa Redblacks. *(1802)*

Politics and Law

Lynn Toler, lawye and judge best known as the arbitrator on the television series *Divorce Court.* *(1959)*

James Carville, American political commentator and strategist known for his work on the presidential campaign of Bill Clinton and for co-hosting several television news and commentary programs. *(1944)*

Funmilayo Ransome-Kuti, Nigerian women's rights activist known as "The Mother of Africa." *(1900)*

Funmilayo Ransome-Kuti (courtesy UNESCO)

Journalism and Letters

Anne Tyler, best-selling novelist, famous for *The Accidental Tourist, Breathing Lessons,* and other works. *(1941)*

John Berryman, American poet and scholar best known for his Pulitzer Prize-winning *The Dream Songs.* *(1914)*

Henry Steele Commager, American historian best known for his 1950 book *The American Mind* and numerous other works. *(1902)*

Thomas Macauley, British historian and essayist known for his multi-volume *The History of England* (1848) and the poem "Horatius at the Bridge." Also served as Secretary of War and Paymaster-General during the reign of Queen Victoria *(1800)*

Military

Klaus Barbie, SS captain and Gestapo member known as the "Butcher of Lyon." *(1913)*

Music

Ciara, singer-songwriter whose debut album *Goodies* earned four Grammy nominations. *(1985)*

Katy Perry, singer-songwriter whose breakthrough hit was the 2008 single "I Kissed a Girl." *(1984)*

Chely Wright, country music singer and gay rights activist known for her hits "Shut Up and Drive" and "Single White Female." *(1970)*

Ed Robertson, lead singer, guitarist, and songwriter of the rock band Barenaked Ladies. *(1970)*

Chad Smith, drummer for the Red Hot Chili Peppers, member of the Rock and Roll Hall of Fame. *(1961)*

Chrissy Amphlett, singer-songwriter with the Divinyls, known for their 1991 single "I Touch Myself," which she co-wrote. *(1959)*

Jon Anderson, singer-songwriter best known as the lead vocalist of Yes and for his collaborations with Vangelis. *(1944)*

Helen Reddy, singer known for the 1971 hit "I Am Woman." *(1941)*

Roberto Menescal, Brazilian musician important in the development of bossa nova. *(1937)*

Earl Palmer, rock and blues drummer and session musician inducted into the Rock and Roll Hall of Fame. *(1924)*

Eddie Lang, musician widely regarded as the father of jazz guitar, member of the Big Band and Jazz Hall of Fame and the Grammy Hall of Fame. *(1902)*

Georges Bizet, French composer known for his opera *Carmen* and other works. *(1838)*

Helen Reddy

Johann Strauss II, composer known as "The Waltz King," whose compositions include "The Blue Danube" and "Tales from the Vienna Woods." *(1825)*

Performing Arts

Josh Henderson, best known for his lead role as John Ross Ewing III in the 2012 revival of the television series *Dallas. (1981)*

Mehcad Brooks, actor known for his roles in the television series *Desperate Housewives, The Game, Necessary Roughness,* and *Supergirl. (1980)*

Sarah Thompson, actress best known as Eve in the television series *Angel* and Rose in *7th Heaven. (1979)*

Craig Robinson, actor known for his role as Darryl in the US version of The Office, and for various supporting film roles. *(1971)*

Mathieu Amalric, French actor and filmmaker best known as the lead villain in the 2008 James Bond film *Quantum of Solace. (1965)*

Michael Boatman, actor known for his roles on the television series *Spin City, China Beach,* and *Arli$$. (1964)*

Tracy Nelson, actress, daughter of singer Ricky Nelson and granddaughter of Ozzie and Harriet Nelson. *(1963)*

Johann Strauss II, by Fritz Luckhardt (1899)

Nancy Cartwright, best known as the voice of Bart on the long-running animated series *The Simpsons.* (1957)

Eugene "Porky" Lee, child actor known for the *Our Gang/Little Rascals* comedies; originated the catchphrase "O-tay!" *(1933)*

Marion Ross, film and television actress best known for her role as Marion Cunningham on the sitcom *Happy Days. (1928)*

Tony Franciosa, actor who played the leading roles in five television series, including *The Name of the Game* and *Finder of Lost Loves. (1928)*

Jeanne Cooper, played Katherine Chancellor on the soap opera *The Young and the Restless* from 1973 to 2013, mother of actor Corbin Bernsen. *(1928)*

Billy Barty, television and film actor known for his short stature (3'9"). *(1924)*

Minnie Pearl, country comedienne known for her long tenure on the Grand Ole Opry and the TV series *Hee Haw. (1912)*

Abel Gance, French director in the silent film era, particularly known for his monumental 1927 film *Napoléon. (1889)*

Leo G. Carroll, English actor known for his roles in several Hitchcock films and for the television series *The Man from U.N.C.L.E. (1886)*

Minnie Pearl

Leo G. Carroll (right, with bottle) as Alexander Waverly in *The Man from U.N.C.L.E.*

Philosophy and Psychology

Lawrence Kohlberg, American psychologist best known for his theory of the stages of moral development. *(1927)*

Max Stirner, German philosopher important in the development of nihilism and individual anarchism, made early contributions to psychoanalytic theory. *(1806)*

Religion

Father Coughlin, Roman Catholic priest and political leader famous for his radio broadcasts featuring anti-semitism and opposition to FDR. *(1889)*

Science

William Higinbotham, physicist on the team that developed the first nuclear bomb, also created the first interactive analog computer game using a graphical display. *(1910)*

Sports

Fabian Hambüchen, German gymnast who won a gold medal at the 2016 Olympic Games. *(1987)*

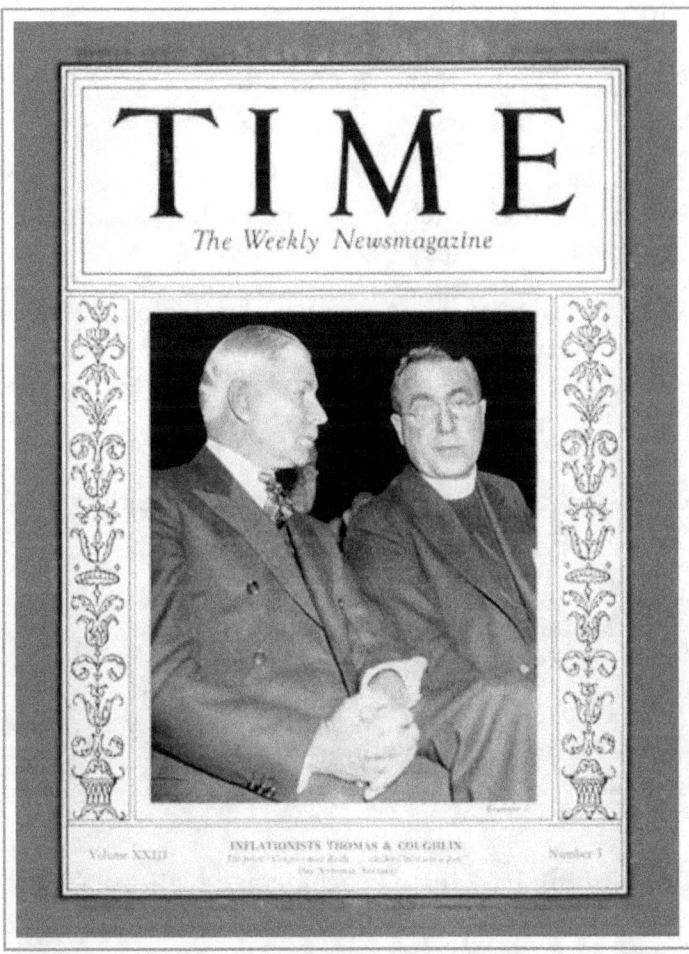

Father Charles Coughlin (right) with US Senator Elmer Thomas on the cover of *TIME* magazine, January 15, 1934

Rosa Mendes, WWE wrestler and model who was a cast member on the E! reality series *Total Divas.* *(1979)*

Kateryna Serebrianska (Катерина Серебрянська), Ukrainian gymnast who won a gold medal at the 1966 Olympics. *(1977)*

Pedro Martínez, pitcher with the Boston Red Sox, member of the Baseball Hall of Fame. *(1971)*

Mike Eruzione, ice hockey player best known as captain of the US national team that defeated the Soviet Union in the 1980 Winter Olympics, known as the "Miracle on Ice" game. *(1954)*

Dan Issel, basketball player and coach, member of the Basketball Hall of Fame and the College Basketball Hall of Fame. *(1948)*

Dan Gable, wrestler and coach who won a gold medal in the 1972 Munich Olympics. *(1948)*

Dave Cowens, basketball player and coach inducted into the Naismith Memorial Basketball Hall of Fame. *(1948)*

Bob Knight, basketball coach named National Coach of the Year four times, known for his volatile temper, famously throwing a chair across the court during a game. *(1940)*

"Smokin'" Joe Mercer, English jockey who rode a career total of 2,810 winners, received the Order of the British Empire. *(1934)*

Dan Issel

Bobby Thomson, baseball player who made the pennant-winning three-run home run for the New York Giants in 1951, known in baseball history as the "Shot Heard 'Round the World." *(1923)*

1948 Bowman Gum card of Bobby Thomson

Lee MacPhail, baseball executive, son of Larry MacPhail, also a baseball executive. Together, they are the only father-and-son pair to be inducted into the Baseball Hall of Fame. *(1917)*

Jack Kent Cooke, entrepreneur and owner of the Washington Redskins, the Los Angeles Lakers, and other teams. *(1912)*

Smokey Joe Wood, pitcher and outfielder for the Boston Red Sox and Cleveland Indians, known for his fastball. *(1889)*

1912 American Tobacco Company card of Smokey Joe Wood

Bat Masterson (Photo: Robert Marr Wright)

Who Died on October 25?

Adventure and Exploration

Bat Masterson, iconic Wild West buffalo hunter, Indian fighter, lawman, and gambler; inspiration for the 1958-1961 television series *Bat Masterson. (1921)*

Crime and Punishment

Albert Anastasia, Cosa Nostra mobster who helped found the American Mafia and Murder, Inc. *(1957)*

Military and War

Kara Hultgreen, first female carrier-based fighter pilot in the US Navy. *(1994)*

Sadako Sasaki (佐々木 禎子), famous hibakusha (bomb-affected person) who was two years old in Hiroshima when the US dropped the atomic bomb. She died at the age of 12 from radiation-induced leukemia, and is known for folding 1,000 origami cranes, which according to Japanese legend will grant the folder a wish. *(1955)* *(Photo next page)*

Sadako Sasaki

Music

Jack Bruce, singer-songwriter and bassist best known as a member of Cream. *(2014)*

Roger Miller, singer-songwriter best known for his novelty hits including "King of the Road," "Dang Me," and "England Swings." *(1992)*

Bill Graham, impresario and promoter who founded the Fillmore and Fillmore East rock venues. *(1991)*

Virgil Fox, organist whose "heavy organ" Bach concerts aimed at teaching rock fans to appreciate classical music.. *(1980)*

Performing Arts

Marcia Wallace, actress best known for playing Carol on the 1970s TV sitcom *The Bob Newhart Show.* (2013)

Hal Needham, film director and stunt man known for his collaborations with Burt Reynolds, including *Smokey and the Bandit* and *The Cannonball Run.* (2013)

Gerard Damiano, directed the cult classics *Deep Throat* and *The Devil in Miss Jones.* (2008)

Richard Harris, actor known for such films as *Camelot, A Man Called Horse, Unforgiven,* and for playing Dumbledore in the first two Harry Potter films, as well as for his 1968 recording "MacArthur Park. *(2002)*

Viveca Lindfors, Swedish actress in numerous films and television series. *(1995)*

Mildred Natwick, actress in such films as *The Trouble With Harry, Barefoot in the Park,* and numerous television roles. *(1994)*

Vincent Price, actor particularly known for horror films. *(1993)*

Vincent Price in *House on Haunted Hill (*1959)

Forrest Tucker, appeared in nearly a hundred films, best remembered for his role in the TV sitcom *F Troop. (1986)*

Cleo Moore, Hollywood blonde bombshell and cult favorite known as "Queen of the B-Movie Bad Girls." *(1957)*

Poetry and Literature

Jacques Barzun, historian whose 1945 book *Teacher in America* shaped the schoolteaching profession. Awarded the Presidential Medal of Freedom and the French Legion of Honor. *(2012)*

Mary McCarthy, novelist and critic best remembered for her 1963 best-seller *The Group. (1989)*

Lord Dunsany, writer known for his fantasy novels, especially 1924's *The King of Elfland's Daughter,* also chess and pistol-shooting champion of Ireland. *(1957)*

Frank Norris, journalist and novelist known for *McTeague* (made into the classic Erich von Stroheim film *Greed*), *The Octopus: A Story of California,* and *The Pit. (1902)*

Geoffrey Chaucer, greatest English poet of the Middle Ages, famous for *The Canterbury Tales. (1400)*

Science and Technology

Harry Ferguson, engineer and inventor known for his role in developing the modern tractor, first person in Great Britain to build and fly his own airplane, and developed the first four-wheel drive Formula One car. *(1960)*

Evangelista Torricelli, Italian physicist and mathematician best known as the inventor of the barometer. *(1647)*

Sports

Bill Sharman, basketball player and coach, two-time inductee into the Naismith Memorial Basketball Hall of Fame, once as a player and once as a coach. *(2013)*

Emanuel Steward, trained 41 world champion boxers, member of the International Boxing Hall of Fame and the World Boxing Hall of Fame. *(2012)*

Wellington Mara, influential in the development of the National Football League, co-owned the New York Giants. *(2005)*

Payne Stewart, championship golfer, member of the World Golf Hall of Fame. *(1999)*

Bobby Riggs, World No. 1 tennis player, best known for his challenge match against Billie Jean King in the "Battle of the Sexes" match. *(1995)*

Abebe Bikila (አበበ ቢቂላ), Ethiopian famous for winning a gold medal in the 1960 Olympics marathon event while running barefoot. *(1973)*

Willie Anderson, first golfer to win four US Opens, member of the World Golf Hall of Fame. *(1910)*

Abebe Bikila running barefoot in the 1960 Olympic Games
marathon even

Quote of the Day

"A man doesn't begin to attain wisdom until he recognizes that he is no longer indispensable. "

Admiral Richard E. Byrd,
polar explorer, born October 25, 1888

Holidays Around the World

October 25

For INTERNATIONAL ARTISTS DAY: "An Artist's Studio," by
Thomas Rowlandson. (1814)

Holidays Around the World

If you're looking for a reason to take your special day off, you should know that every single day is a holiday somewhere in the world! Here's some of what you can celebrate on October 25!

General Events

Armed Forces Day (Romania)

The nation of Romania honors its military on October 25, because on this day in 1944, the Romanian Army liberated the last Romanian city under Nazi occupation.

Day of the Basque Country (Basque Country)

The Basque Country, an autonomous community in northern Spain, celebrates the passing of the Statute of Autonomy on October 25, 1979, granting it certain national rights.

International Artists Day (worldwide)

Launched in 2004, International Artists Day honors the contribution artists make to society each October 25.

Retrocession Day (Taiwan)

Commemorates the end of fifty years of Japanese rule and return to self-rule on October 25, 1945.

Sovereignty Day (Slovenia)
Commemorates the withdrawal of the last Yugoslav People's Army soldier from its territory on October 25, 1991, a key event in the process of Slovenian independence.

Thanksgiving Day (Grenada)
Thanksgiving Day in Grenada is a national holiday marking the anniversary of the US-led invasion of the island on October 25, 1983, to depose its then-current government.

Food Holidays

In the United States, almost every day of the year is dedicated to a particular food. (Some other countries do this also, but not every day.) Sponsored by manufacturers, retailers, farmers, or simply fans, these days are often proclaimed by the President, Congress, state governors, or mayors. Given that there are more different foods than days of the year, some days honor more than one kind of food!

In the US, October 25 is **National Greasy Foods Day**. While greasy foods definitely aren't healthy, they are quite tasty. Eat them in moderation year-around, but perhaps today is a day to splurge!

Elsewhere, it's **World Pasta Day,** the creation of the World Pasta Congress held in Rome on October 25, 1995, to promote the "economic feasibility, gastronomic versatility and nutritional value of pasta."

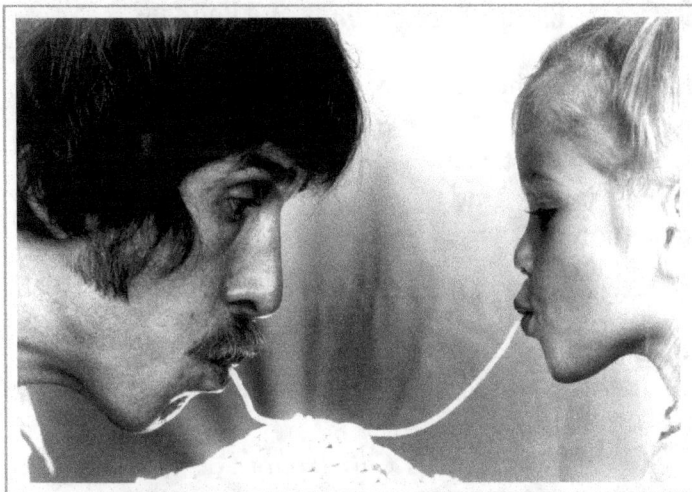

For WORLD PASTA DAY: Musician Peter Alsop and a child eating spaghetti (Photo: Moose School Productions, CC BY-SA 4.0)

In addition, the entire month of October is used to celebrate numerous foods. Here's a list of what to eat in the month of October!

- National Apple Month
- National Applejack Month
- National Caramel Month
- National Cookie Month
- National Dessert Month
- National Pasta Month
- National Pickled Peppers Month
- National Pizza Month
- National Popcorn Poppin' Month
- National Pork Month
- National Pretzel Month
- National Seafood Month

Christian Feast Days and Holidays

Each day in the year is considered a feast day for one or more saints. They are somewhat different in western Christianity (Catholicism and many forms of Protestantism) and in eastern (Orthodox) Christianity. There are many others; this is a selection.

In *Western Christianity*, it is the feast day of Saints Crysanthus and Daria, Crispin and Crispinian, Gaudentius of Brescia, Minias of Florence, and Mar Nestorius.

In *Eastern Orthodox Christianity*, it is also the commemoration of Martyrs Marcian and Martyrius of Constantinople, the Righteous Saint Tabitha (widow raised from the dead by the Apostle Peter), and Anastasius the Fuller.

Moveable and Multi-Day Events

Some events take place over a specific week or time period. Start and finish dates may vary from year to year. Some events occur on different days each year (such as "fourth Saturday of a month"). These events sometimes take place on October 25.

Fourth Monday (10/22-28)
- Labour Day (New Zealand)

Last Monday (10/25-31)
- October Bank Holiday (Ireland)

Last Friday (10/25-31)
- Nevada Day (Nevada)
- Teacher's Day (Australia)

October Honorary Months

Presidents, Congresses, and nations around the world issue proclamations recognizing particular months to honor certain causes. These events generally fall in October, though honorary months do come and go. Holidays established by states and nonprofit organizations are listed if verified. If not otherwise specified, all months are US. There is some variation from year to year; some celebratory months get added and others get dropped. Two places to get up to date information are the current edition of *Chase's Calendar of Events* or the website Brownielocks. Here are some honorary designations for October.

Culture

- Black History Month (UK)
- Filipino American History Month
- German American Heritage Month (September 15-October 15 in the US)
- Hispanic Heritage Month (September 15-October 15 in the US)
- Italian American Heritage Month
- LGBT History Month
- Polish American Heritage Month

Health

- American Pharmacists Month
- Brain Tumor Awareness Month (Canada)
- Breast Cancer Awareness Month

- Dental Hygiene Month
- Down Syndrome Awareness Month
- Dwarfism/Little People Awareness Month
- Dyslexia Awareness Month
- Eczema Awareness Month
- Health Literacy Month
- Healthy Lung Month
- Infertility Awareness Month
- Liver Awareness Month
- Medical Ultrasound Awareness Month
- Physical Therapy Month
- Spina Bifida Awareness Month
- Sudden Infant Death Syndrome (SIDS) Awareness Month
- World Blindness Awareness Month

Other

- Bat Appreciation Month
- Black Speculative Fiction Month
- Caffeine Addiction Recovery Month
- Church Library Month
- Class Reunion Month
- Domestic Violence Awareness Month
- Fair Trade Month
- Feral Hog Month
- Financial Planning Month
- International Walk to School Month
- National Adopt a Shelter Dog Month
- National Arts and Humanities Month

Just for Fun

Anybody can make up a holiday, and many people do! While none of these are officially recognized and some may come and go, here are a few more holidays for October 25.

- National Chucky, the Notorious Killer Doll Day (based on the popular horror film series)
- Sourest Day

October, by Morburre

Quote of the Day

"I'm so glad I live in a world where there are Octobers. "

Lucy Maud Montgomery
in *Anne of Green Gables*

About
the
Month
of

October

"October" from the *Brevarium Grimani* by Simon Bening (c.1510)

October: The Tenth Month

The sweet calm sunshine of October, now
Warms the low spot; upon its grassy mould
The purple oak-leaf falls; the birchen bough
Drops its bright spoil like arrow-heads of gold.

— *"October," William Cullen Bryant*

In Latin, *octo* means eight, so it may seem odd that October is actually the tenth month! The reason goes back to the early Roman calendar, which began the new year in March. What about January and February? They didn't exist, because winter was considered a "monthless" period. Those two months didn't join the calendar until 713 BCE, pushing October from eighth to tenth in the calendar year.

Whether it's the eighth or the tenth month, October has always had 31 days. The last day of October and the last day of February end on the same day of the week in both regular and leap years.

From a seasonal point of view, October is the second month of autumn in the Northern Hemisphere and the second month of spring Down Under. October is the equivalent of April in the other hemisphere.

As an odd bit of trivia, more US presidents have been born in October than any other month: John Adams, Rutherford B. Hayes, Chester A. Arthur, Theodore Roosevelt, and Jimmy Carter.

October in Other Cultures

The month of October has different names in different
languages. Some are very similar to English (octobre,
oktober, etc.), while some are quite different. Some nations
use calendars other than the Gregorian, and their months
may overlap with October. In lunar-based calendars, such as
the Islamic calendar, months move through the seasons, but
many of these languages have a word for October.

Albanian: Tetor

Anglo-Saxon: Wyn-monath (wine month)

Arabic (Egypt, Sudan, Yemen): يونأغينافبرايتشرين
الأَأكتُوبر (uktūbar)

Arabic (Levant): حزيركانوشباتشرين الأُول (tishrīn al-
awwal)

Arabic (Libya): الصهناالنالتمور، الثمور (at-tumūr; al-
tumūr)

Arabic (Morocco, Algeria, and Tunisia):
جأَيفيفرأَكتوبر، أُوكتوبر (uktūbər; ūktūbər)

Azerbaijani: Oktyabrı

Basque: Urri

Chinese: 十月 (Cantonese: sahpyuht; Mandarin:
shíyuè; Taiwanese: chap-goeh)

Croatian: Listopad

Czech: říjen

Finnish: Lokakuu

Greek: Οκτώβριος (Októbrios)

Haitian Creole: Oktòb

Hebrew: ינפבבראוקטובר (ôqtôber)

Hindi: अक्टूबर (aktūbar)

Irish (Gaelic): Deireadh Fómhair mí Dheireadh Fómhair

Italian: Ottobre

Japanese (traditional calendar): 十月 (jūgatsu); 神無月 (kaminaduki)

Khoekhoe (Nama): ǂnûǁnâiseb

Korean: 시월 (siweol)

Lithuanian: Spalis

Manx: Jerrey-fouyir

Maori: Whiringa ā nuku

Old English: Winterfylleþ

Polish: Październik

Quechua: Kantarayki

Russian: октябрь (oktjabr')

Sardinian: Ladàmini

Scottish Gaelic: an t-Sultain

Sesotho: Mphalane

Spanish: Febrero

Swahili: Oktoba

Swazi: iMphala

Thai: Tulakhom

Turkish: Ekim

Ukrainian: жовтень (zhovten)

Vietnamese: 胐迣 (tháng mười)

Welsh: Hydref

Yiddish: פֿעברואַאָקטאָבער (oktober)

Zulu: uOkthoba

October Sayings and Superstitions

Here are some sayings and superstitions associated with the month of October.

October Weather Superstitions

Rain in October means wind in December.

When birds and badgers are fat in October, expect a cold winter.

When berries are many in October, beware a hard winter.

If ducks do slide at Hallowtide, at Christmas they will swim; if ducks do swim at Hallowtide, at Christmas they will slide.

There will always be 29 fine days in October.

If the October moon comes without frost, expect no frost till the moon of November.

Halloween Superstitions

If you see bats flying around your house on Halloween, ghosts and spirits are nearby.

If you go to a crossroads at Halloween and listen to the wind, you will learn all the most important things that will befall you during the next twelve months.

Children born on Halloween are said to have the gift of second sight, and can ward off evil spirits.

If you see a spider on Halloween night, it means the spirit of a departed loved one is watching over you.

If you ring bells on Halloween, you will chase away evil spirits.

And if you want to meet a witch, put your clothes on inside out and walk backwards on Halloween night!

October Wedding Superstitions

If in October you do marry, love will come but riches tarry.

The three luckiest months for a wedding are June, October, and December.

An October bride will be pretty, coquettish, loving, but jealous.

Married when leaves in October thin, toil and hardships for you begin.

October Symbols

Birthstones by Culture: Although a variety of birthstones have been associated with each month, the National Association of Jewelers adopted an official list of stones for each birth month. For October, the stones are *opal* and *tourmaline*.

Other stones associated with October include *aquamarine* and *coral*. There are also birthstones associated with the signs of the zodiac. For October, Libra (9/23-10/23) is associated with *chrysolite*, and Scorpio (10/24-11/21) with *beryl*.

Birth Flowers: *Calendula,* also known as *Marigold*, or Cosmos. It is associated with warmth, elegance, and devotion, as well as comfort and healing.

Birth Tree: The ancient Druids associated trees with different months of the year. For people born between September 30 and October 27, the birth tree is *ivy*. From October 28 through November 24, it is the *reed*.

"October," by Eugène Grasset

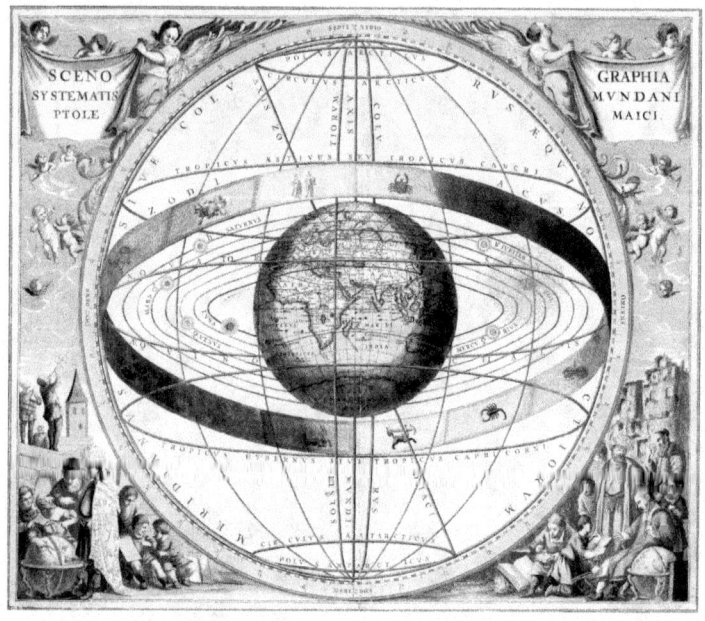

Scenography of the Ptolemaic Cosmography, by Johannes van
Loon, based on Andreas Cellarius's *Harmonia Macrocosmica,* 1660

October 25 Zodiac Signs

From the perspective of someone on Earth, the Sun appears to move through the sky throughout the year, along a path astronomers call the *ecliptic plane*. The ecliptic plane is divided into twelve constellations, known as the zodiac, based on traditionally observed patterns of stars. On your birthday, you can't see your constellation, because it's in the daytime sky.

The zodiac was first developed by Babylonian astronomers about 2,500 years ago. Because they were unaware that the Earth wobbles like a spinning top (known as *precession*), they didn't make allowance for the fact that the Sun's path through the zodiac changes over time.

That means there are now two sets of dates for your birth sign. The *tropical dates* are the original Babylonian dates; the *sidereal dates* tell you where the Sun actually appears as it moves along its annual path.

For October 25, the tropical sign is **Scorpio** and the sidereal sign is **Libra**

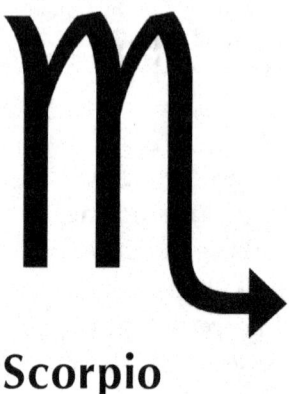

Scorpio

Tropical October 23 to November 21

Sidereal November 16 to December 15

Scorpio, the Scorpion, appears in the Greek myth of the hunter Orion. Because Orion had touched the robes of the goddess Artemis, in revenge, the goddess had the scorpion kill Orion. As a reward, she placed the scorpion in the sky, where it chases Orion through the eternal night.

Scorpio is a fire sign, and people born under this sign are supposed to be determined, reserved, loyal, and secretive. Scorpios are supposed to be compatible with the water signs of Pisces and Capricorn.

Libra

Tropical September 23 to October 23

Sidereal October 16 to November 15

The Babylonians considered Libra, the Scales, to be sacred to the sun god Shamash, patron of truth and justice. The Romans reassigned the scales to Astraea, the celestial virgin, better known as Virgo.

Libra is an air sign, and people born under this sign are supposed to be extroverts, socially graceful, and just. Librans are supposed to be compatible with the other air signs of Gemini and Aquarius.

Illustration by Edward Penfield

What Day of the Week is October 25?

On what day of the week does October 25 fall?

Surprisingly, this isn't an easy question. Because the calendar year is 365 days long (366 in leap years), it doesn't divide evenly by the seven days of the week.

Also, the Earth goes around the Sun in about 365-1/4 days, so a calendar tends to drift over time. That's why the same date falls on different weekdays in different years.

This is made even more complicated by a change in calendars that took place in 1582. Our modern calendar has its roots in ancient Rome, in a calendar reform conducted by Julius Caesar. Caesar commissioned mathematicians to attack the problem, and they came up with the idea of leap years, and thus standardized the calendar for centuries to come. This was called the Julian calendar.

Over time, however, the small errors in Caesar's calculation compounded. That's why Pope Gregory XIII commissioned the Gregorian calendar, used in most of the world today. Some countries converted in 1582, when the calendar was first developed; some converted later; other still haven't changed.

Gregorian and Julian aren't the only types of calendars. The Hebrew year, the Islamic year, and many other calendars are used in different parts of the world and among different people.

You can convert Gregorian dates to other calendars, including the Hebrew calendar, the Islamic calendar, and even the Mayan calendar by visiting the Fourmilab Calendar Converter at http://www.fourmilab.ch/documents/calendar/.

Chinese calendar systems are quite complex and have changed several times; a full discussion is far beyond the scope of this book. If you're interested, you can find information here: http://www.hermetic.ch/cal_stud/chinese_cal.htm.

On Names and Dates

Historians use "CE" (Common Era) and "BCE" (Before the Common Era) instead of the more common "AD" (Anno Domini, or Year of Our Lord) and "BC" (Before Christ), reflecting the fact that the year-numbering system established by the Gregorian calendar is used throughout the world in many countries not culturally Christian.

The CE/BCE designation dates back to at least 1708, and has been adopted as a standard by the United Nations and the Universal Postal Union. Because this series of books covers events and people of all nations and cultures, we use the CE/BCE terms.

The abbreviation "O.S." ("Old Style") on some dates refers to the fact that the Russian Empire did not switch from the Julian to the Gregorian calendar at the same time as the rest of Europe, and therefore some figures and events have two dates.

Also, in the Julian calendar in England in the 16th century, the year began on March 25 rather than January 1. To avoid confusion with Gregorian dates, dates between January and March were often written using both years.

People and events whose original names are not in the Western alphabet have their native names (where possible) in the appropriate script shown in parenthesis. If you are using an e-reader to access an electronic version of this book, all characters don't always display on all devices.

A 50-year brass perpetual calendar.

Quote of the Day

"Time is an illusion, lunchtime doubly so."

Douglas Adams,
from *The Hitchhiker's Guide to the Galaxy*

Notes
and
Credits

THE 12
ACC—
MAGNA

Timespinner
Press

Cartoon by John T. McCutcheon

Copyright, Credit, and Contact

Follow Us

Our blog "This Day in History" (http://
timespinnerpress.com/this-day-in-history/) features short
articles on events and people associated with each day, and
updates several times each week. Also subscribe to the
"Quote of the Day" at http://timespinnerpress.com/quote-
of-the-day/. You can get daily links by following us on
Facebook at TimespinnerPress, or on Twitter as
@sidewisethinker.

Contact Us

Find an error or a format problem? Want information about
the series, about us, or about when the volume for your
special day might be available? Please email us at
editor@timespinnerpress.com. (We also take requests if your
special day isn't yet complete. Please give us at least six
weeks' notice if possible.)

Sources

We owe a great debt to Wikipedia, which is our first stop for
research. We attempt to make independent confirmation of
all important dates and facts through a variety of other
sources.

Other sources we frequently use include the Library of
Congress; "on this day" listings from *Encyclopedia Britannica*,
the *New York Times*, and the BBC; Omniglot for the names of
months in other languages; *Chase's Calendar of Events*; and, of
course, the always essential Google.

All art and photographs are either in the public domain, used under a Creative Commons license, or with a "fair use" justification, and most frequently come from Wikimedia Commons and the Library of Congress Prints and Photographs Division.

Attribution is provided where possible, or as requested by the copyright owner, or when there is particular historical significance, listed below. For information about any particular illustration or photograph, please contact us.

Credits

1. The illustration "Charge of the Light Cavalry Brigade, 25th October 1854, under Major General the Earl of Cardigan," was created by William Simpson and E. Walker in 1855, and is in the public domain because its copyright has expired.

2. The illustration of the month of October used on the back cover is from the French Gothic illuminated manuscript *Les Très Riches Heures du duc de Berry* by the Limbourg Brothers, Jean Colombe, and an intermediate painter whose name is lost to history. It is in the public domain because its copyright has expired.

3. The box graphic used on the first page is from a 1916 pamphlet entitled "Divorce versus Democracy" authored by G. K. Chesterton, originally published in London by the Society of St. Peter and St. Paul. It is in the public domain in the US because it was published prior to 1923, and is in the public domain in all countries (including the country of origin) in which the copyright time is the author's life plus 70 years or less.

4. The graphic design for the section pages in this book is from a design originally created for a pharmacy label. It is courtesy of Wellcome Images (ICV No 11073, photo V0010813), and is used here under CC BY-SA 4.0.

5. The painting "The Charge of the Light Brigade" by Caton Woodville is in the public domain because its copyright has

expired. The original is located in the Palacio Ral de Madrid, Spain.

6. The timeline of the Charge of the Light Brigade was developed for the book *Forgotten Heroes: The Charge of the Light Brigade*. It has been released into the public domain by its authors.

7. The poem "The Charge of the Light Brigade," by Alfred, Lord Tennyson, is in the public domain because its copyright has expired.

8. The 1915 illustration of King Henry V at the Battle of Agincourt is by Harry Payne. It is in the public domain because its copyright has expired.

9. The map of the Battle of Leyte Gulf was originally published in the US Navy's *All Hands* magazine, December 1944 issue. It is in the public domain as a work created by a sailor or employee of the US Navy as part of that person's official duties.

10. The 1912 portrait of Pablo Picasso by Juan Gris is in the public domain in the US because it was created prior to January 1, 1923, and is in the public domain in its country of origin and other countries and areas where the copyright term is the creator's life plus 80 years or less.

11. The poster for the 1930 film *With Byrd at the South Pole* is in the public domain because it was first published in the United States between 1923 and 1977 without a copyright notice.

12. The 2014 photograph of Funmilayo Ransome-Kuti is courtesy of UNESCO, and is used here under CC BY-SA 3.0.

13. The 1975 publicity photograph of Helen Reddy is in the public domain because it was published in the United States between 1923 and 1977 and without a copyright notice. Traditionally, publicity photographs are not copyrighted because of the way in which they are intended to be used.

14. The 1899 photograph of Johann Strauss II by Fritz Luckhardt is courtesy of the Gallica Digital Library (ID btv1b8453822q). It is in the public domain because its copyright has expired.

15. The publicity photograph of Minnie Pearl was taken between 1965 and 1972, is in the public domain because it was published in the United States between 1923 and 1977

and without a copyright notice. Traditionally, publicity photographs are not copyrighted because of the way in which they are intended to be used.

16. The 1967 publicity photograph from *The Man from U.N.C.L.E.* is in the public domain because it was published in the United States between 1923 and 1977 and without a copyright notice. Traditionally, publicity photographs are not copyrighted because of the way in which they are intended to be used.

17. The January 15, 1934, cover of *TIME* magazine is in the public domain because copyright was not renewed on many early issues of the magazine.

18. The photograph of Dan Issel is courtesy Sport Magazine Archives. It is in the public domain because it was first published in the United States between 1923 and 1977 without a copyright notice.

19. The Bowman Gum card of Bobby Thomson is n the public domain because it was first published in the United States between 1923 and 1963, and although there may or may not have been a copyright notice, the copyright was not renewed.

20. The 1912 American Tobacco Company baseball card of Smokey Joe Wood is in the public domain because it was first published prior to January 1, 1923.

21. According to Japanese Copyright Law the copyright on the 1955 photograph of Sadako Sasaki has expired and is as such public domain.

22. The cropped screenshot of Vincent Price in the 1959 film *House on Haunted Hill* is in the public domain because it was first published in the United States between 1923 and 1963, and although there may or may not have been a copyright notice, the copyright was not renewed.

23. The 1960 photograph of Abebe Bikila is in the public domain in its country of origin because it was first published in Italy and its term of copyright has expired under the Law for the Protection of Copyright and Neighbouring Rights n.633, 22 April 1941. The image has been cropped.

24. The 1814 watercolor "An Artist's Studio" by Thomas Rowlandson is in the public domain because its copyright has expired. The file is courtesy Google Art Project.

25. The 2016 photograph of Peter Alsop eating spaghetti with a child is by Moose School Productions, and is used here under CC BY-SA 4.0.

26. The graphic "Le mois d'octobre, église de Bagnot" is by Morburre, and is used here under CC By-SA 3.0.

27. The painting "October" is from the Brevarium Grimani, circa 1510, and is in the public domain because its copyright has expired.

28. The 1815 woodcut of a proposal is in the public domain because its copyright has expired.

29. The 1896 drawing "October" by Eugène Grasset is in the public domain because its copyright has expired.

30. The celestial sphere is from *Scenography of the Ptolemaic Cosmography,* by Johannes van Loon, based on Andreas Cellarius's *Harmonia Macrocosmica,* 1660. It is in the public domain because its copyright has expired.

31. The 1906 automobile calendar is by Edward Penfield, and is in the collection of the Library of Congress Prints and Photographs Division. It is in the public domain because its copyright has expired.

32. The 50-year perpetual calendar photograph is in the public domain.

33. The cartoon by John T. McCutcheon is from his 1905 collection *The Mysterious Stranger and Other Cartoons by John T. McCutcheon.* It is in the public domain because its copyright has expired.

License Description and Terms

Aside from material purely in the public domain, photographs and other material in this book are used under specific licenses permitting free use, usually with an attribution requirement. For full text and terms of these licenses, click or enter the appropriate links below. If you believe there is an error in the copyright status or attribution of any of these images, please email us.

- Creative Commons Attribution 2.0 Generic (CC-BY 2.0): http://creativecommons.org/licenses/by/2.0/deed.en

- Creative Commons Attribution-Share Alike 3.0 Generic (CC-BY-SA 3.0): http://creativecommons.org/licenses/by-sa/3.0/

- Creative Commons Attribution-Share Alike 2.5 Generic (CC-BY-SA 2.5): http://creativecommons.org/licenses/by-sa/2.5/deed.en

- Creative Commons Attribution-Share Alike 2.0 Generic (CC-BY-SA 2.0): http://creativecommons.org/licenses/by/2.0/deed.en

- Creative Commons Attribution-Share Alike 1.0 Generic (CC-BY-SA 1.0): http://creativecommons.org/licenses/by-sa/1.0/deed.en

- CC0 1.0 Universal (CC0 1.0) Public Domain Dedication (CC0 1.0) http://creativecommons.org/publicdomain/zero/1.0/deed.en

- GNU Free Documentation License (GFDL): http://en.wikipedia.org/wiki/Wikipedia:Text_of_the_GNU_Free_Documentation_License

- License Art Libre (Free Art License): http://artlibre.org

Timespinner
Press

Other Books from Timespinner Press

The Story of a Special Day
Michael Dobson

A series of (eventually) 366 volumes covering everything that happened on your special day! Events, births, deaths, quotes, holidays, and much more. It's like a birthday card they'll never throw away!

US$7.95 print/US$2.99 ebook.

From Plassey to Pakistan
Humayun Mirza

The history of British Colonial India and the formation of Pakistan from the unique perspective of the son of Pakistan's first president and last of the royal line of Bengal, Bihar, and Orissa! This unique historical document tells the inside story of this distinguished family, including the detailed story of the coup that toppled his father from power!

US$27.95 print

A Whole New Navy: America's War in the Pacific

Miles Durr

The most comprehensive and detailed description of America's naval war in the Pacific ever—every battle, every ship, every task force and every task group from Pearl Harbor through the Japanese surrender! A must-have for the collection of every World War II buff!

US$29.95 print

Improbable History: The Weird, the Obscure, and the Strangely Important

edited by Michael Dobson

From the birth of Western civilization to the rescue of Apollo 13, from the Leaning Tower of Pisa to Florence's Duomo, history has often turned on small, improbable details. Whatever happened to the ancient Samaritan people? Why did a fortuitous rainstorm allow the British to conquer India? How did an air raid in Italy lead to the development of chemotherapy? What happened when Albert Einstein met Adolf Hitler on the streets of Berlin? How did the Japanese manage to attack the US mainland using balloons? A cast of award-winning writers tackle some of the strangest tales in history!

US$19.95 print